T0102673

LOGBOOK WRITTEN BY A DRIFTER

Poetry Collection

Tendai Rinos Mwanaka

Mwanaka Media and Publishing Pvt Ltd,
Chitungwiza Zimbabwe

Creativity, Wisdom and Beauty
Publisher:

Mmap

Mwanaka Media and Publishing Pvt Ltd

24 Svosve Road, Zengeza 1

Chitungwiza Zimbabwe

mwanaka@yahoo.com

https//mwanakamediaandpublishing.weebly.com

Distributed in and outside N. America by African Books Collective

orders@africanbookscollective.com

www.africanbookscollective.com

ISBN: 978-0-7974-8615-7

EAN: 9780797486157

© Tendai Rinos Mwanaka 2018

All rights reserved.

No part of this book may be reproduced or transmitted in any form or by any means, mechanical or electronic, including photocopying and recording, or be stored in any information storage or retrieval system, without written permission from the publisher

DISCLAIMER

All views expressed in this publication are those of the author and do not necessarily reflect the views of *Mmap*.

Contents Table

Introduction

Logbook written by a drifter, is a cycle of interlinked poems that deal with life, spiritual aspects, language, philosophical ideas and love relationships in their various levels, or depths, but focuses more on a relationships that has changed the character; that the character doesn't know how to deal with, that has make the character into some sort of a wreck, emotionally, psychologically, or even spiritual, especially spiritual. The character is both telling himself that he doesn't want the girl, he wants her, he can live without her, and he can't live without her. It is this confusing aspect, the indecisiveness, the want to know the truth, the inner need to want to find someone we can connect to, this obsessive want, that drives us as we drift through this emotional roller coaster.

The poems in this collection touches on early adult coming-of-age love poems, love poems in a world in the shadow of the AIDS pandemic, our dire need as humans to want to connect our lives to someone, especially now in the 21st century, and how mostly, it is ending in break-ups and disillusionment, the psychological, spiritual and emotional wreck one can be when dealing with a failed relationship. The poems are in bits and dribs, of different people connecting to this issue, love, talking... Telling their own love stories, in their own way thus I don't always use the conventional modes of poetry. In this attempt, I am allowed to explore a range of poetic liberties, devices and techniques in having the characters in the poems stamp their own emotions on the page. It is very experimental, challenging and incisive, thus it has the ability to look a subject straight in eyes without flinching.

Sometimes the poems are fractured, jagged, with phrases disappearing off the edges. I have the mixing of many different styles and genres (diary, essays, notes, sketches, philosophical discourse, rants, chants etc...) with the poetic genre. There are poems that are in parts, and I try to connect these parts, coming on one after another.

Poems in *Logbook written by a drifter* touches on most aspects of love; falling for a girl or boy (their meeting), enjoying the goodness of a relationship (kissing), breakdown of a relationship (Too many years later), sex (careless lovers). There are those that deals with love as an image or a poet's constructs (love on this page), loss (Tear on my surface), death (Half knowing, half not knowing), memories (Stars), hope, wistfully (Calling for you), and the far pervading sense of identity (My life), spirituality or spiritual wreck (Jewellery), philosophical (undertaking zen), life (October moon) and language (every twisted word); thus they create a broad range of feelings world; living, loving and being. There are different types, forms and structures of these poems in this collection. Some forms of tanka, sonnets, long poems, chants, rants, notes, sketches, prose poems, essay poems, almost-story poems, experimenting with Germany's dichten denken (poetry and thought), echo poetry, wordplay, ekphrasis, dreams, daydreams, abnormal states of mind (like the beat generation poems), and any other erratic inclinations are explored.

What am I attempting to achieve with this collection. *Logbook written by a drifter* records life, emotions and the feelings the character is drifting through, as he deals with a love unfulfilled. He is in a small space, like the space between a hard place and a rock, and he thus makes that space his own. The collection encourages us to keep those spaces, spaces of the drift, until we have dealt with the hard elements and or the rock elements, and everything is alright again. Sometimes drifting is all we can do!

logbook written by a drifter

How can I undo what I did?
To make it less painful
to un-stress myself
To fit in, to pass in, to slip
through the invisible boundary
that has kept us strangers

How can I put it best?
without laughing at my past
A debris of junked life, like a
logbook written by a drifter
Seeking and sighting heaven!

For you were everything that I never
was, would ever be
Everything you had always wished
that I had been
Everything the reflection you found
so coincidental is really years
of your constructions.
Making me a martyr of your
ideologies, not less than that!

Only to turn my life into an abalone shell

And like dry grass,
I was broken
I felt like a box
I had no power to close
neither to open myself

So that I could be able to tell you
the things that I never dared
Because I didn't think
you cared

Wishing I could go back
and undo
this blemish of our past.

untitled

i could be dead
i could be alive
all that doesn't matter
i am here is what matters
alive or dead.

Half knowing, half not knowing

December's last sighs of
December's sun, like us
is beyond our territory's stiff netting
Towards the sun's fast setting
We mark this time, evening
as we dip our tapping toes
into Friday's noisy tolls

Night time is a beckoning look
trying to beat the clock
as it turns into dusk
In the final heat fanned
by the last of the sun's fingers
Casting complexions of wagging tails
Shadows of no colours
Night yawns in the expanse of stars-
Dims, quells, sinks, deletes-

Electing this quite night
Impatient darkness furious
Scoffs at my refusal
To walk with him, an angry
brushy fire, his hunger is smoky
He says my end is down
The little dirty road, a bit down
Promising me that he will be back

Life is too mathematical
Wandering through my casual
Everyday brain's trading
On my mind, a score tricks.
Trying to learn how not to
Half knowing, half not knowing
How to catch it before it tells me
To try to cancel it

But still bracing upto his face
A face without a name
The strangest among us
Has to push his string far
A make-believe string frayed
And hallowed by absence
Above all of our heads
For us to get past the scales
That asks not for permission
And lead the frightened children.

Untitled

where there is no choice
we deal with what
we did not choose
and choose what we
do not want to choose.

every twisted word

The way words explain
but do not explore
themselves....

It's like the way words
collect into a phrase,
that has never before
existed.

The way what has
been mapped
wearing big,
ideas like clothes
can never flash
into the unknown.

Moving again,
this hand is
with the sun.
As words discover
the meaning
that defines the natural
good in all of us.

More picture,
less word
this fractured lettering

is the language
of this hand.

The lightness of
the hand
is gone
only the madness
gains.

Every twisted word here,
nonsense!

rumour written on the wind

wet with dust
the wind is
unleashing
wind-racking
passions
unraveling spools
of wire-flung
into the sky,
shivering
on top of
an open sky
into spaces

opaque
merry-go
rounds
debauched,
tree's branches
stripped naked
by dismal
demented
Augusts' winds

And in the pools
of dust
the windows
are wrapped

As we spent
Noon hours
in windy
afternoons
walking on top
of yellow leaves,

The wind, slicing
fiercely,
the burn of
the wind
on our eyes
, almost
protecting us
like next of kin.

Rumour
written
on the wind
whispering of
no wind-holes
offered
of ante-bellum
gentry
gone to the south
In the hazards
of the wind's
swishes.

love on this page

love, a hug
speaking
a thumping voice in my heart

exclaiming slowly
exclamation marks
in lighting the first star
are not punctual

punctuation marks
do not answer
question marks
of her untwisting heart

i am her footnote
when did I become this?
but she is still the text
a shredded cloud
re-gilding my heart

stripped
in my mind, of
all things necessary

i am a new text with strange

symbols
odd signposts;
i twirl in rapids.

stars

My love had the melody
of the stars in it
Weeping spirit bones
of the stars.

Shinning silver nogal.
Shinning so brightly.

Cold as a vacant heart,
her heart was ice
and blue,
stars in cold black
empty skies.

In the half light of the stars
the smooth grey stones
of my heart.

were like those stars
that breaks
against the dark
nights.

tiny insect vessels
of great hope
longing for the light!

even dying for it,
hating it
like the moth
on a fire.

time

Desire names this place
possessive about panic
like a shadow of time.

Prone to heart's murmurs
shift shapes of desires
wagging through this time.

Storing this time
like sunshine
into our own skins.

Our eyes pressed
to the keyholes
of our lives.

Time runs down
our spines
like a shiver.

As we rub seconds,
minutes, and hours
One against the other.

The friction
propelling us
forward.

Time falls apart
and breaks
into a puzzle.

Measuring this time.
by the mix of
these elements

Is that a poor
attempt at
timekeeping?

silence

The uncertainties we house
as silence
resounds inside us

In its own time,
not ours
flexing silent wings

We are surprised
by the parts
that are imperceptible

Each has its own space
before it falls to a sleep
in silence outside silence.

Yeti on K2 Mountain

Licking
the clouds,
the mountain
K2 Mountain
defines you
and you define
the mountain
Munching
the sky for it.

The only
question here
would be effort's
answers
to the mountain's
questions.

tear on my surface

Love thriving in her human carriage.
A vessel that contained
The love that already existed
And we were lovers snarling
Through parsecs of love-bites.
Touching each other's heart with gold

Her glance seemed to have tasted the wind.
And she knew she had placed her love.
In front of pain and sorrow.
She knew she would die from this
Dying like the heart's wings closing.
The way the heart's wings closes

Her love losing its breath in the bottom
Of my heart's bottomless canals.
Her love scattering into dust
Her voice like broken shards of glass.
Like rosettes of pain.

Parts of her face are still water
She left a drop on my surface.
A scar on the skin of things
Her hand still poking into my heart
Like clothes that echoes into the skin.
Even in secret places

And now that she is gone
Her humidity soaks everywhere I go.
Like mist in the valleys of my mind.
And I am thinking of her
Longing to hold her in my arms.

Standing with an open heart
Weeping oceans of eternal emotions
I know I love her, I love her physically!
And now I know that love is always
Shallow until it's ensconced into our souls.

rain

The sky is steel grey and mackerel...
Some clouds wings are black-ringed
Some clouds are white-fringed

Dark and white clouds
Snagging in darkening metaphors
Battling in lightening metaphors

The dark grey fevers of the clouds
beginning their own lives
In the rains locked in a battle
of a song of mud and season

In the afternoon that is
dripping into evening
With the fading day's light
of the sun, out and hidden
Behind the clouds but still
prozacking its way to night's fall

The lonely mountain's eye
licks the sky
The mountain eats away
at those crazy clouds
And in the colourless part of me
I am like the mountain's eye
a sponge in the rain

This dance of lively thoughts
are rich rhythms of speech
Like needles of the raindrops
that are boundaries
sparkling in the fading day's light

The rain repeats the stencils
of their loud vowels
thick as paste on the windows
Setting life free!
And the earth's page
Coloured by these rains
has turned green.

october moon

October moon arrives at my door
A little ghost, raw orangey zest
The chaff of the moon floods the valley
With pale yellowish flowers of light
And melting slivers, breathing coolness!

The slivers of the bright moon rocks
The ashes below heaven, down
With heat that is warm to touch.
Its half rim like a distant fire
Is burning the eastern horizons.

We might as well think we are
yellow-throated
In the moonlight's pouring cornlight

Listening for our names
In the million-petalled slivers
of the moon's being
Unbowed by life's winds
The moon has pulled over us
like a Cyclops's eye
In the long silences the moon collects.

Pushing night into dawn
dawn into morning
The night's eluding face

slipping away with a quite
Undressing the moon
Spherical arc in death
Emerging Eve, imaging
naked and embarrassed!

my life

My life a tessellation
of colours
Collecting light like candles
My life a shift
of sound, breath drifting
As if through a lick
something gathered inside

My life the beginning of sound
Sweet, soft and spherical-
Slouching raindrops, distant
Slow noises, vowels, almost loud
My life fast-beating sloshes of light
creating haloes
Sometimes hard strings humming

I am busy doing the work for the ashes
They have already scattered
In the scleroderma
Of my puny soul skulking

My life fading gaslamps
fading at daybreak
Like some things
some magical things
that are meant to stay
And if you take apart their pieces

they would sift away
sieving away like lost memory

My life a conflict
The wound that simply watches you
My life a pen dropped in a well
Angels that have no choices

The well's waters will come out
cleaning the slate for me
to imprint the road
that I am travelling in
And I can't block my road
because it is the only way
to go home
And it is time to go home

My life question marks
Is staying out ever content
to stay away, to live without?
My life anonymous blood
in anonymous veins and arteries

Being in a world of contradictions
balancing the known
with the unknown
For an instant I lose the telling
I feel the quite entering
And stiffly, I crawl inside my mind

relieving myself from speech

My life the physical feelings
Inside the emotional worlds of words
When words must remain wordless
When words would draw you in

My life the power of the body
That makes us, defines us, explains us
Into such fine specimens

Do you want me to be you?
And discard being me
Do you really think I will?
Mistake you for me
Insane of you!

My life the skeleton everyone
Hates, is scared of
Like driving, dodging cows in the road
as if valkyries are haunting me
My life the blood in trees
Inside the rings of waiting trees

Empires of emptiness I rule
and have. You can't see
The sandy neoprene or the silence
passing in the clusters
of these hesitations

My life travelling through
memory mazes
So many amazing
Memories that have lost meanings
The years and memories
being finally abandoned
Sloughing on the table like
common junk.

My life a simple
Formulae, calculations of
additions and subtractions
And it turns out this answer
is suddenly snoot-smeared
By our deeds
or lack of which

My life the life of soil
Layers and layers of soul
that tells and manifests
My life the soul on fire
Clinging to cognition
in luminal spaces

And man is a prismatic showing
Of possibilities of the divine
Qualities being shared bringing
people into generative humanity

and beingness of totality

My life imperfectible
unperfected
destined to be perfect

My life the tune
is the end of the line
Have I listened to my tune?
Torn asunder out of my life
Or have I answered my call?
Or re-invented someone's tune?

too many years later

You are brooding on a sun's absorbing obsidian rock, besides the ocean. It's been many years. You are trying to admit to something. Its meaning is blocked from you by that fat luminous light some folks call the sun, up there in the beautiful skies. How come this ocean you are staring at is vanishing into itself: how come the ocean is emptying onto the beach and, emptying away into itself, without an explanation or a reason for that? You are still calling out to someone in the long deep notes as of the bluesy guitar, as if still expecting an answer, calling as if from the deep pit of the ocean. Where does the ocean's hole goes when it is filled up with water? Your answer, "I think..." feathers itself into a soft moan, no words coming after it. These moans float away into the blue skies, into air, into a story. And when you utter out your answer, where are the words going? Where do the sounds really go? It's not even an answer you are going to tell with words and gestures but with sounds, each tiny sound, a tiny marker. You still remember what it was like to pursue someone helplessly in the rain, in the dark of the summer nights, and to relive that moment too many times, too many years later. Loneliness to you now is that you are not even here.

broken connections

She was a woman
A woman of actions
She lived on the front
Filling me with fantasies
Sensations I can't contemplate
Without ecstasies

She was the reasons
She was the justifications
Of my being
Of all that I have ever done

But her laughter drives
Inwards of me
To teach me lessons
Of broken connections

calling for you
for Robin Perry, this is your life story

everyday that we live
we throw pebbles into the pool
and the pebbles create ripples
someday the ripples would meet.

you say you are leaving me today.
we are sixteen, young and immature.
coz in our hearts we know we have to let go.
in my heart i know, i can't let you go.
in your heart you know, we were never meant to be.
in our hearts we know, we have to marry others

this is our safety net
that someday
i would come for you

can i glimpse the map that's sending you away.
can i feel the price you are paying now.
can't delay you, to help me escape.
our hearts touches the pure silence between us.
could only think of you, on and off over the years.
but she left me after thirty years.
and i knew it was time to call for you

goggled your name on the net, the rest is history.
left Phoenix Arizona for Toowoomba Australia.

mailed out my love to the address of your heart.
Rod Stewart sang *First cut is the deepest*
i believe it's true, that we belong together

this is my heart's call
that today
that's calling for you

at all times respect your heart's potential by following your pat
through your heart.

step strongly into your eternal sunset, for a push can bring us out o
our calling in a lifetime contrived by time.

but the mountain is calling us to its peak again and our callin
becomes another calling; another calling, and another calling...

neighbours

Time itches to be whirled away between here and there whilst listening to the eyes of neighbours, setting down the patterns of our small lives. They chatter and laugh and cackle angrily like a blue jay at our leaf shadows. Their scripts, of our lives, read aloud in their stupid spats, their strangely words fluting the right or wrong of us doing this and that. Eating these neighbours' words is simply a dumb exercise for their words only narrows to just a few chats.

Tony Katzew vs. MND

the MND is saying to Tony

"i don't have a head or tail. you cannot
beat me for i am going to destroy you.
give up, and i will take you peacefully"

and Tony now has anger and vulnerability to keep
himself on course. And all he can do now is to use
his brain to fight it. For the rest of his body is dead.

he has learned only one art; "to compartmentalize
his thoughts or mind or else he will be full
of thoughts, 24hrs a day."

Tony now has many compartments: death,
his son in Cape town; lectures, happy memories;
problems..., his wife who left him?

"if i want to laugh, or analyse fear, i just open
the right one." he now lives in a virtual world of
"safety-deposit-boxes." and at night he closes of
all compartments, take pills and go to sleep.

Tony's voice is starting to strain, is rough and slowing
down his speech, forcing him to stumble over long words.

one vocal cord has been killed by motor neurone

disease (MND). And the idea of falling silent terrifies him
but its part of his journey, its part of his battle with MND.

Tony is preparing to use mouth operated computer
to communicate, but eventually his lungs will collapse
and his body will switch-off and darkness will overcome him
like every winter leaf has to fall.

but when light switches on again, when the leaves sprout
on winter trees, when he dies, he says, he hopes
"to find answers to why the disease chose him."

autumn

Forward to a reddish autumn
Multi-layered, multi-
coloured paths
Emblems of our archetypes

And metaphors
of our times
Unthinkable parameters
If colours could swap?

thembi ngubane's dream

"Hello HIV,
you trespasser!
You are in my body.
You have to obey the rules.
You have to respect me.

And if you don't hurt me,
i won't hurt you.
And if you mind your business,
i will mind mine.

Then i will give you a ticket-
when your time comes."

making love to 4 walls

You said, "Kill your mother!"
And you will take care of me
I did that. I crossed the ocean
for you on foot, no ship
could get me across. I reached
the stars for you, without an
aeroplane. Carrying the moon
for you. In my hands, holding
your insides in my hands. Step
on step, carrying the lice's ass.
We were belt and trousers. For
you I was your mirror. But now
you are gone: a fly fallen into
the beaker full of milk. Our sphere
is now a torn cloud, a buffalo's
carcass. My love for you has
flown away. Your face is now a fairy
tale to me. Every night I make love
to 4 walls like a widow. I don't
garner respect anymore, like the
wind, like the newly wed breaking
into tears. You gave me a huge
whack on the face. You left me with
no credit. You now sleep out like a
winter cow. The drums beating saying,
"you, you, you." They never say,
"her, her, her." The drums

made from leopard's skin.
The drums, that's the drums
you were listening for, waiting for.
They make you enter the dance floors.
And they are saying to you, "give
him beer." All the beers, you get drunk.
The beer swallows you. You swallow
money with the small houses {mistresses}.
It's a cup with its own sweetness.
You open your mouth, wider.
To drink from this cup, so delicious
like fish's soup, even old man will go fishing.
Your tongue, let it stay
in its kraal. It's not a calm body
part. Where we meet no grass will
grow. For I am now a blank sky.
An angry bachelor, rejected. When
you see me create friendship with
the wind, running, let the legs break.
You can buy a new pair. My brain is
now my husband, lover..., crossing me
into a relationship. If spinsterhood stinks
let the flies follow me. Let them eat me...

kissing

Constructing a meeting with her
She weaves an appearance
Allowing the impossibility to enter
South winds of desire rising
Ready to snuggle in cotton candy dreams

She kisses you: brown lips
Dark honey, the sweet lips
Dripped in spit like a newborn thing
Her tongue pushing in, bequeathing
Assaulting each other with love
Your heart is caught on her lips

Your cold, ideal slowly melting
Under her hot particulars
While the moon-red, soft
Inevitable, sizzles around you
It is a full moon rolling down
The stairs, like a heavenly
Body, gliding, crashing onto
The earth, the light, the weight
Of its heat pressing layers
Of your flesh down.

A deeply planted splendour
Burns beneath your breast
You are a teenager bursting

Into his surprising body,
Headlong and you, alive to the light
Telling you of steps to be taken

When the kissing consumes you
You face each other
With vengeance, ripped
Each other's clothes, rolled
Around in the dirty
And make love like animals

So she is born, and you watch
Born of men, born in need
In lust that is in love
You are her world, she is yours
You have a partner for anything
Competition, copulation
Cooperation, conversation?

undertaking Zen

How could I store this material…
On this page, freezing myself from
Unlearned meaning maps?

Zen has a corner flea market
On human nature's connections
With human mind, the human
Greys that prickles, perks at
Some things, you have salvaged
Through a haphazard life.

Since you are aware of
Yourself as a unique moment
Then appearance is no different
Than desire and inspires
Intuition, that is more invaluable
Than valuable knowledge.

These human lies are only
Shadows of the real truths
That human nature knows
What it doesn't know
And it doesn't know
And tells what it knows
Tell me, how can that harms
Even if it is not true?

You know you are now the major
Of your own body, a decorated captain
Of a well-lived body, loved, learning
From the sharp cuts, jags, nags
You are just a general coming
To sad manhood.

Hush now! The universe
Assembles itself
If you ask me, I will tell you the truth!
That, it's me who is really wrong!

Sluices of meanings show
Balm of naked honesty
Painful with words that make
No meanings, information is
The only key component in
This language game.

multi-tasking

You were so pretty to look at
But I shouldn't have picked you
Because being with you was
like waves in a big, ugly ocean
and I was a little boat ploughing
the waves and all you seemed
able to do was to lure me
off-balance

My heart was an accapella solo
still bubbling on
drowning in words
trying to surface
to get you to listen to me
i kept screaming, screaming
that difficulty looked out of you
the way it did.

Whilst your eyes wandered off
you called it multi-tasking
like the morning's example
that's all over,
everywhere
all at once

And I still loved you
like blowing up a float.

so I could not fly though
one breathe warm,
could have set me free.

There was a necessary tearing
where I scissored my heart open
on the painful side of your affections

But like guide out of hurt's
labyrinth.
the rift will seal in time.

careless lovers

Laughter spills like whiskey
From a shot glass
Laughing straight into the sun
We rolled onto the ground
Laughing like the world
Hadn't gone to shit
Song birds, sunrise
Delirious, we fell, a heap of
Careless lovers, invincible
Laughter bouncing from tree to
Tree, in an open sky
Her body split mine
So we lie in copula.
Lovemaking coming in many
Forms: a chime rocks to and from
Tinkling a random wind song
Breaking the memory fragments.

jewellery

I love jewellery
Pearly jewellery
Luminescent jewellery
Dark jewellery
Tiny jewellery
Tinkling jewellery
Jewellery with handles
Jewellery with holes in the
Middle where their hearts
Should be, jewellery
Masquerading as beauty
Jewellery desiring, jewellery
Rejected, jewellery worn-out
I feel the place where jewellery
Have unhinged, was once a part
Of something.

he is here

An echo of the end of time is
The hot amber needle of the wasp
Leaving the house of negation
Open to all.

Leaping wherever he wishes
Foam stretching thin without
A whisper.

Her voice broken
She opens a chasm into the ground
To show that love is
Sutured and abstinent.

their meeting

It just happened
They were walking
In the same road
They did not stop to ask
For better directions
Or thought of separate ways

They did not share notes
Try to understand the methods
To get there or the beginning of things
They never thought of love
It just happened

It was beyond all time even
Though time had other agents
Ivy, stealthy, prising them apart
They did not know at what moment
Time tripped them into abandonment

It just happened
Like two dolphins caught
by the shaft of the moon's light.

The tempers of this light

…on the trees, golden.
Light is massed.
But, I do not
trust.

…its reaches
It reaches
too far into the distant tempers—

Are we just organs of this flight?

Or dramatic fixtures,
Textures,
or settings,

or a conceit, that cannot
be solved?

My words arch,
have no sound
or meaning.

Sub Vocative:
For Norman

Ooe uoi ooo oei eoea
Eoo uii iee ooe eeeio
Aae uioo oeei uiiioeo
Eeoo oiuea aeeiou eui
Aeeeo iouoi eoiuo aeeio

Eouioa
Eiii
Eoiuu
Aooiu
Eiii
Eouioa

Uuuo ioue ooo oie eoia
Eeeiou iiou ioea eouieo
Aeioua eioua eeiiuo eioo
Eaioue eioua eioooe oieai
Eiouaei eiouio euioa eiuoa

Eouioa
Eiii
Eoiuu
Aooiu
Eiii
Eouioa

Ouiae ioueai iuoeaiu iuo
Aeeioui ioue eaiuo ieuoiu
Eiouaei uieoie euioeai eiu
Iouea eiouaie uieouai iuoe
Eiuoe eiuoae euiooe eiiioea

Eouioe
Eiii
Eoiuu
Aooiu
Eiii
Eouioa

goodbye yesterday

Goodbye yesterday, we are now
separated. I have forgotten your
name. I have forgotten my name too
I belong to tomorrow. Don't follow
me. I am a new country. When its
over, it's over. Goodbye yesterday
Today, let's go.

What are you bringing tomorrow?
Come carrying a basket-full
of new things, without yesterday's
troubles. Come now. Don't come
like a chameleon, unassuming...
Strides unsure. I have waited for you
like waiting for a newborn thing.

To be born: its only one day
To celebrate life: we are the work
giving birth, to tears only
We will water our own graves
hitting the earth's lush cheeks
with our own tears.

When a tot, I walked with
four legs. When a teenager
i walked on two legs. Now old
i walk on three legs, on wood

Collecting some firewood. It is
the great blanket of the old
telling stories at night, no fly
will settle on my mouth tonight

I am now the grass the cow
ruminates. I have a frog in
my bowels, eating my insides
I have wasps hiving in my
chest, biting into my lungs,
heart, crickets blurting in my
mind. It's a pointer telling me
the ends of my stories are near

I am what's left behind: a dried
branch of a tree. Let the wood
come to me. I would get
the brush to start my own fire
I don't see where I am going now
I am like mist. Nobody sees me
But I am here, there, everywhere
I feel like going, to go wherever?

I don't want to be put on a
hanger like out of favour dress
Even though I am now a fabric
waiting to be passed down. I am
still thinking with my own heart
like a dog journeying off

to an unknown destination.

Counting the Stars

As I lay by my back at night
Stars scattered in the eastern hem
Do they know each other?
I start counting them
That they might know each other
Only that after a few counts
I begin to drown in the sea of unknown.

Then I start counting again
That this time I might solve this Rubik's Cube
Another has slipped through my mind's fingers
So I start again from the south
Still more sprout from the seams
From that end they seem to march in counting formations.

There is that one a torch among matches.
Promising to keep time until time returns.
Just like Connie, that bright flower
But one day Connie was no more
A mistaken identity, a dark patch stayed
So also stayed, brown-beaten faith
But we grope again, don't we?

We grope again, counting
There is that one dull but countable
Why doesn't it shine to illuminate truth's tracks?
Is it sad and weary of life's never clearing

Thunderstorms of, tsunamis of,
Tragedies, tribulations, trials...
Don't they say?
"Third-degree burns tingles us with respect for the fire?"
Or "stomping the toe makes us more careful of our steps?"

O, where would I place my finger for a new count.
Maybe to the west or to the north
Or, derail the world and its seasons from their tracks
And forget where the tracks are buried.
Whichever way, I have left another
But how many times do we get lost in the maze of our minds.
So many times we forget why the string is tied around our finger.
So many times we are unable to navigate the map.

Haven't we over-looked an erect needle in our chair?
Isn't life a Lego set of?
Both losses and wins, counting
We get down to the table
Can we look back and say
The going has been seamless sailing.
No stops, no stags, no regrets
That we have bagged the big game of-
Everything?

wishes

The writer wishes she was the editor
So she could get all her stories in
The editor wishes he was the writer
That he could write publishable stories

The publisher wishes she was the editor
That she could choose moneymaking stories
The reader wishes he was the main character
That he could be a better protagonist in the story

The main character wishes she was the minor character
That she could hide from the editor's scrutiny
The minor character wishes he was the writer
That he could get the main character's role

And the writer wishes she could never write again
That she might spite all their wishes
But the editor wishes the writer could never stop writing
That he could always find something to lord over

The publisher wishes the editor not to stop editing
That his bank balance would never shrink.

HOME AGAIN

He thought he had taken everything
Maybe he didn't have to think about it
Maybe he really had to leave me
I thought he took away a part of me
I told myself he left with something, mine
But I couldn't ask him not to

He left me an empty blue sky
Dry air is all I could feel inside me
I felt open, like an opening sky
The sun mercilessly pouring hot
No clouds, no air, no breeze
I felt my insides drying, dying
Into a dead, dried, listless bird

He took a side path and left me alone
He left me alone in the lonely road
As I approached the intersection
He left me to die on the cusps of
Something life changing, life taking
He took something that is life giving

It took me years to find out
I had to die inside for me to find
That he hadn't taken anything
That I still had everything inside me
I had to face another loss

My mother dying of Alzheimer
Made me realise what loss really meant

Those bouts of forgetfulness of
My mother's. That she could
Forget me. That she could even
Forget who she was. Where she was
That her death didn't represent loss
For she had nothing more to lose

Made me realise that I hadn't lost
Anything, me or even him. That he
Was the one who had lost me
To find myself again on the road of life
That he had abandoned me in
For me to find myself again
To find my way home again.

WE WAIT AND LINGER, a little

When we were little, stars
The sun, the moon and darkness
Stayed longer as they
Cradled us, as we played

As we grew older
The sun became hotter
Hot we were, in failure
Anxieties and disappointments

And the moon, frail
Faint, it was a grown up
Hiding in the dark skies
Inside houses that were our jails

Now, as we lie isolated
In darkness, immeasurable
Its soft tide pulling us in
We wait and linger, a little

SAD MANHOOD

for Edie... I know how you feel

I am not going to give up on it
Not for anything
Not anything worthwhile

I have come a long way
Some say, half the way
Half the way to sad manhood

For the first twenty years
I was a seed in the soil
Waiting for the rains to spring up

From twenty onwards
I was a sapling stem
Feeding, glowing in greens

Now forty, onwards
I will learn from lives,
Loves I have crashed

To reach here, where
I am just coming to
Half the way to sad manhood.

BEAUTY IS EXISTENCE

Despair through
Beauty
Is oppressive

Despair through
Beauty

It feeds on

Ugliness
Upheavals

Of exiled beauty

We could take
Alms for it

Beauty is
Existence

So go on

Holding it
Beholding it.

SONNET DIPTYCH {Sappho fragment 21 remixes}:
Playing around with "The one with violets in her lap" from Lorraine A. Vail.

She cradles roses in her hands
A sweet smile on her lips
A tremble in her heart, maybe
She waits alone near rock strewn cliffs

      Petals tremble in her hands
      Pale fingers hold fragile stems
      Wind shakes trees-rap, tap, tap
      Breeze moves leaves, her heart pretends

She is not lonely, roses in her hands
Her hair, her skirt, her heart askew
She must be brave, she must adapt
Lost love her heart cannot find

      Roses grown in stone's adapt
      More than roses in her hands

Playing around with "The one with violence in her lap" from Lorraine A. Vail.

She shelters thorns in her heart
 A thorny grin of her teeth
A shudder in her heart, maybe
She sits on vernal dew strewed lawns

Hooked thorns shudder in her heart
Fragile fingers carry thorny stems
Thorns prickle. Limbs are frayed
Wind swirls about, her heart intends

Nothing happened, thorns in her heart
Her lips, her eyes, her teeth smiles
Vultures' swirls, her heart entrapped
She must live this day she will fault

Thorns sown, eternal trap
More than thorns in her heart.

These intimations

She is touching you again
Touch being all of your sight
You step so carefully, so afraid
Of another deep and empty fall
Inwards into another void
If you knock her off-balance
Afraid of grabbing her
Too hard, lingering on the memory
Of why you are still there

Loitering together in the small hours
Holding onto the ropes of tenderness
Trying to reach those glistening
Beaches in each other's hearts
Two moonlit people, you face
Each other, fingers reaching out
Lost in the forests of your delights
Stroking each other's cheeks
Dressing each other with
The clothes of your need.

So much love and
Too many things to do with it
You both love, it seems
From abandonment and need
Perhaps silent, the consolation
Is, not being loved but

Rather you would love
Such extraordinary range
Touching your very human core
You believe in this range
For you to meet.

But she is now gathering you again
To your past, the flagpole of
Your past, asking you to go
And you, you have to go
Like a passing spirit, a genie
Like a dream; you dream
You will dream
You will sip through your dream
And you won't wake up

Your ambition is this
You will stay away
Keeping your secrets hidden
You have to feel nothing
You will stay away
Like rains in the drought year
So that you can only see her light
Brightening up the skies

Casting your image in gold
In the dream you slip, you sleep
Dissolve into its silhouette
And empty out again, bleeding

Spreading yourself out, speeding
Embroider yourself in the effete
Of darkness, in its blackening gullet

Your love is now filled with
The dark blood of your heart
That pulls the heavy ropes
Of your heart, listening, hoping
To hear the answer of
Water, beneath those black
Rocks of fear, in your heart
Sinking to the river bed
Of your heart, disappearing down
It seems into subduction zones
Like oceanic rocks

These intimations, endless as
Raindrops, your road slipping
Away unnoticed. You email
Your heart out to the island
Of her silences. But no dribble
Of your pulse will survive
In your heart, but these intimations.
Hovering in desolate horizons.

Printed in the United States
By Bookmasters